Vol 5

MAZE

Ages 4-6

FOR KIDS

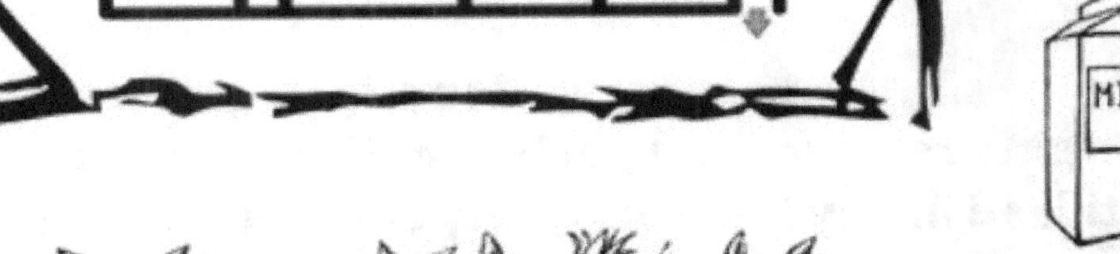

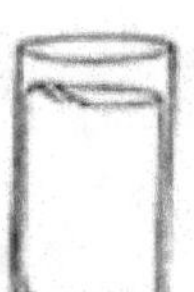

MAZE BOOK

Milk

milk

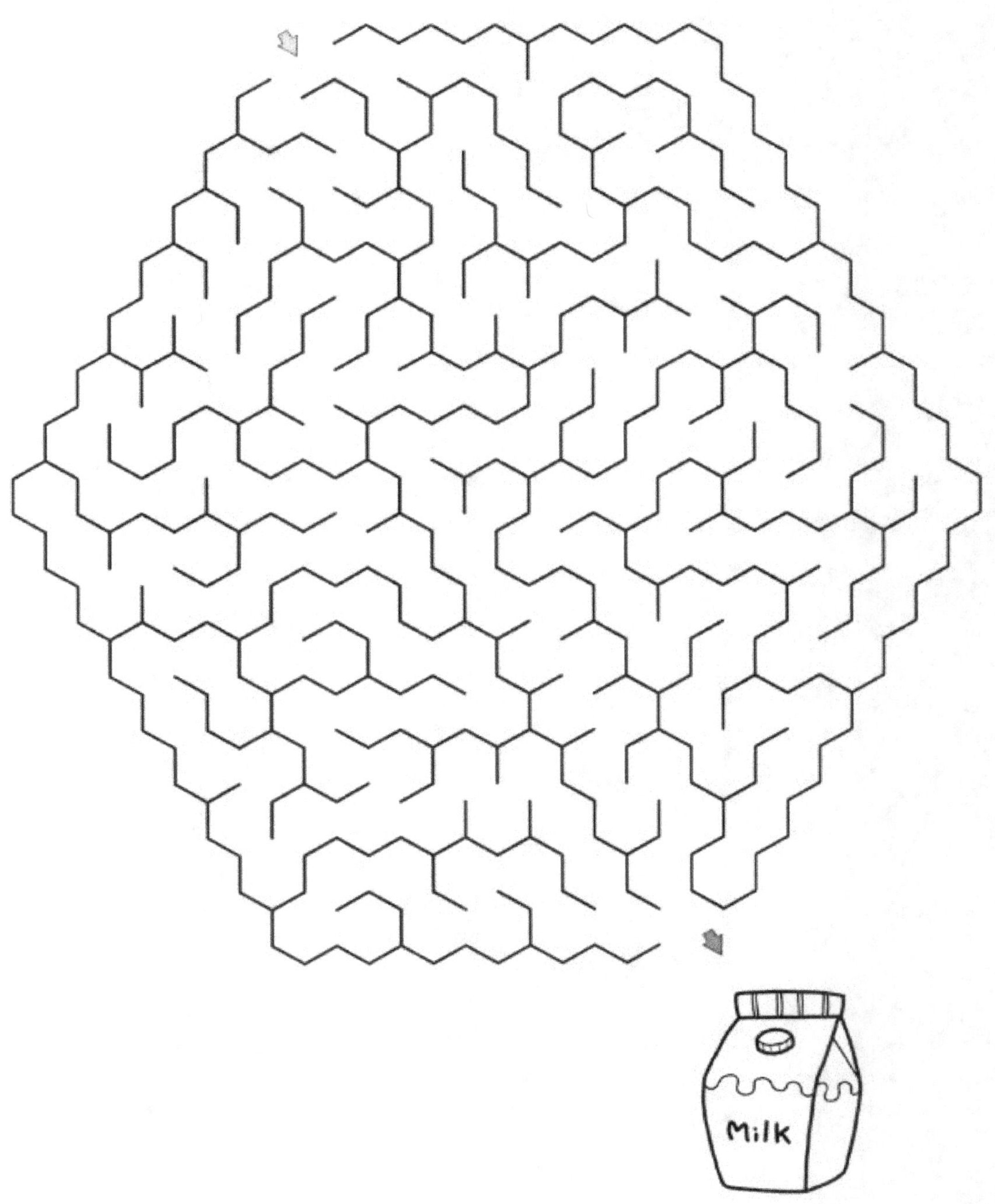

Milk

MILK

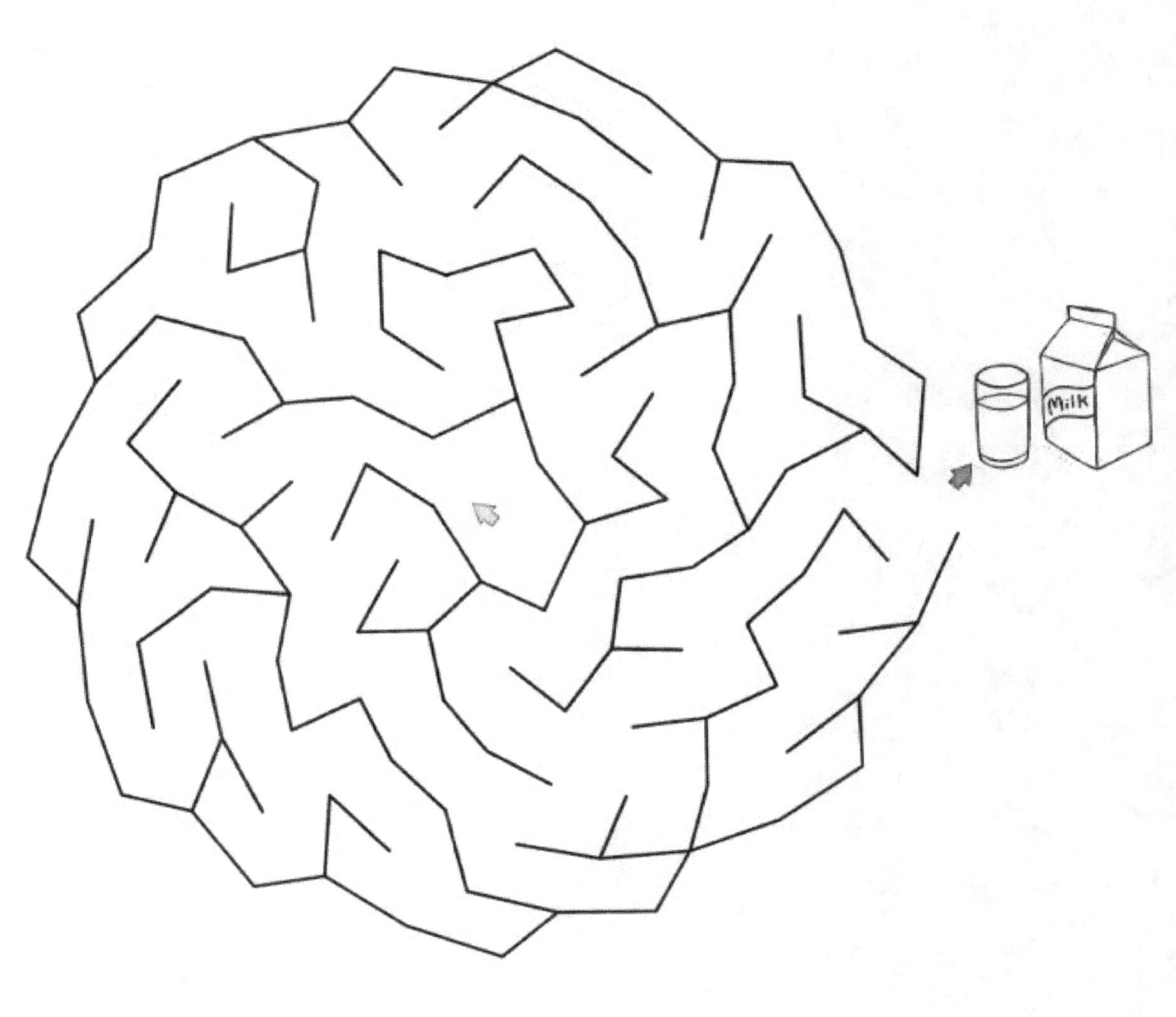
Milk

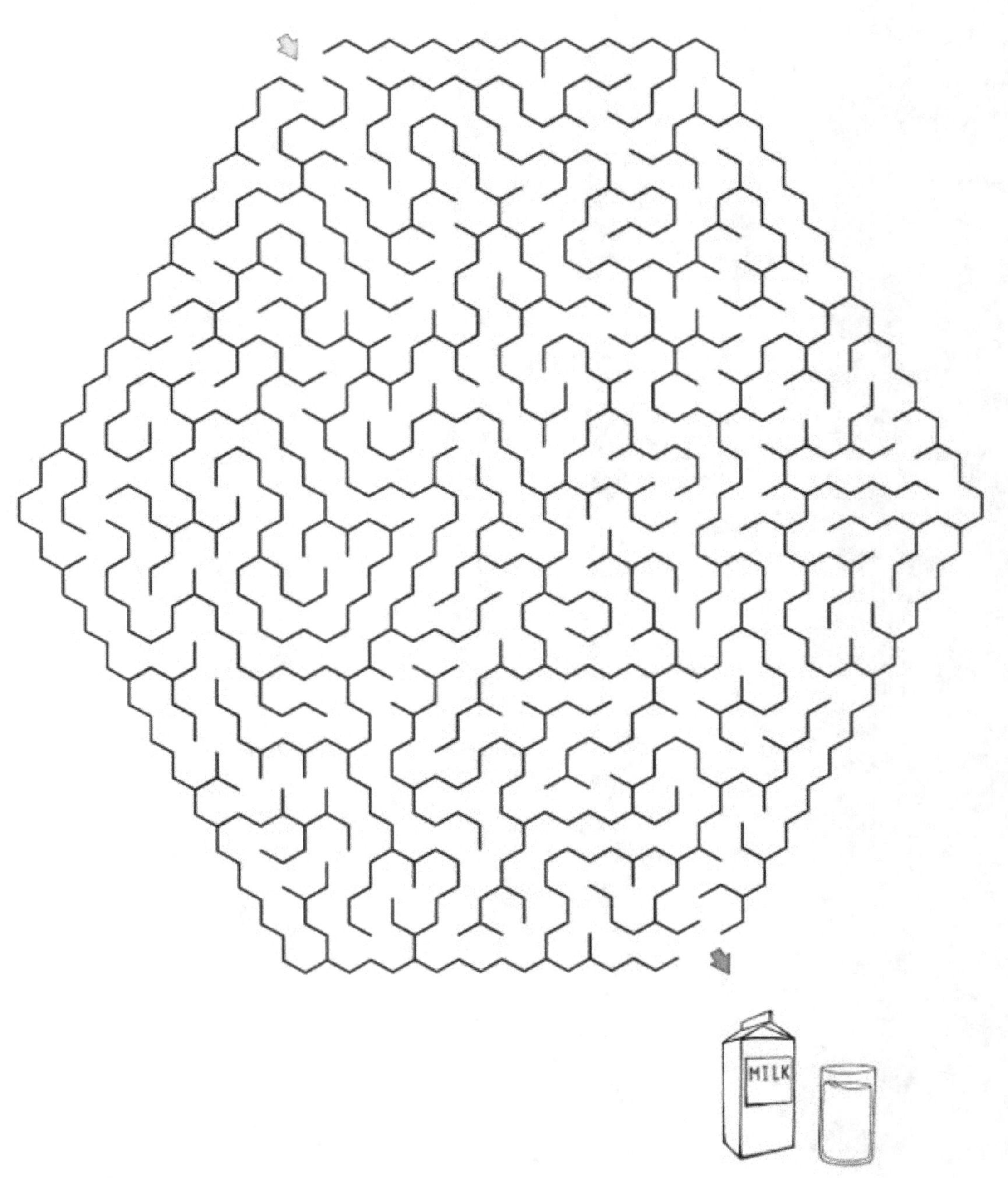

Milk

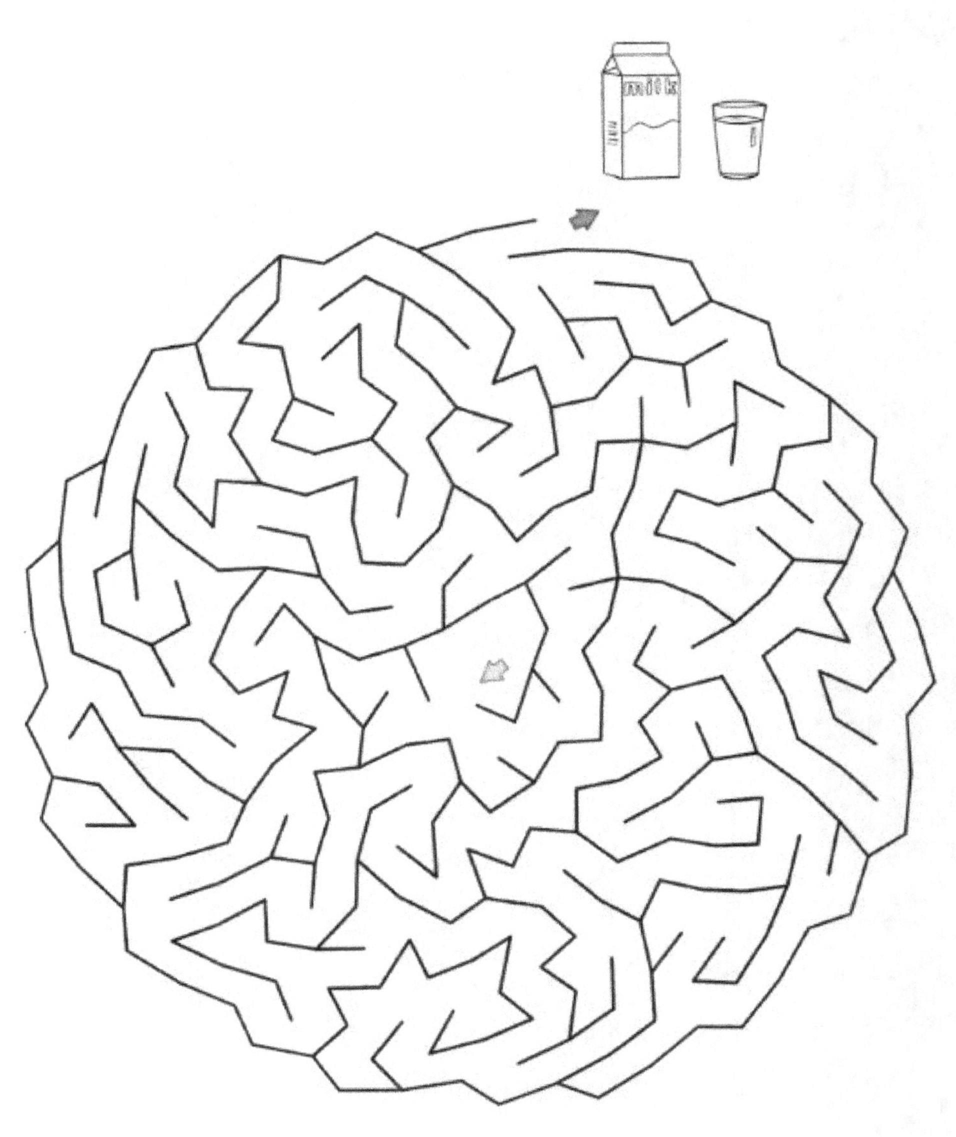

Milk

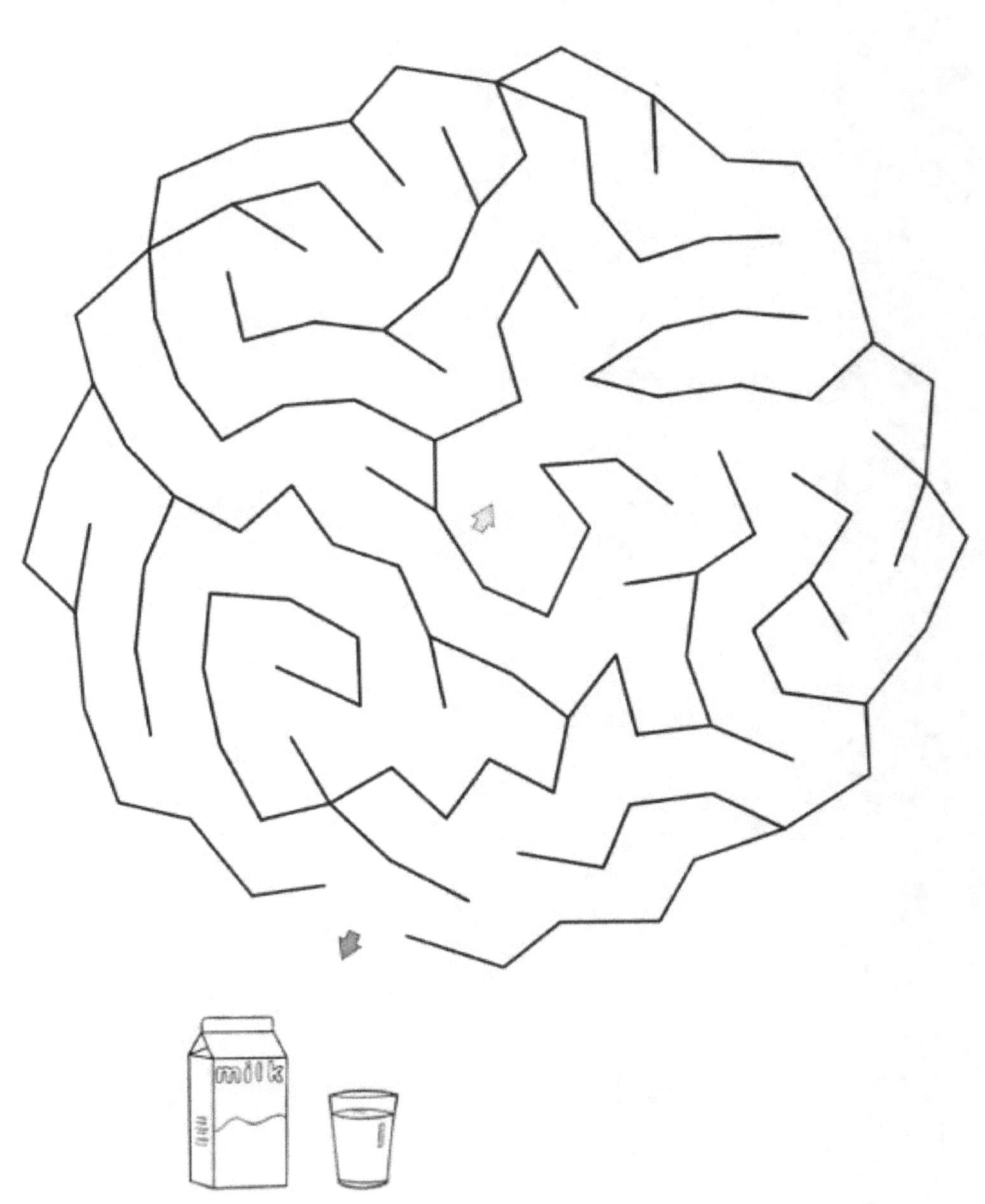

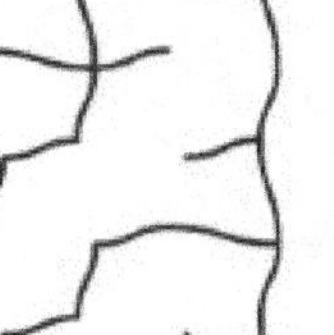

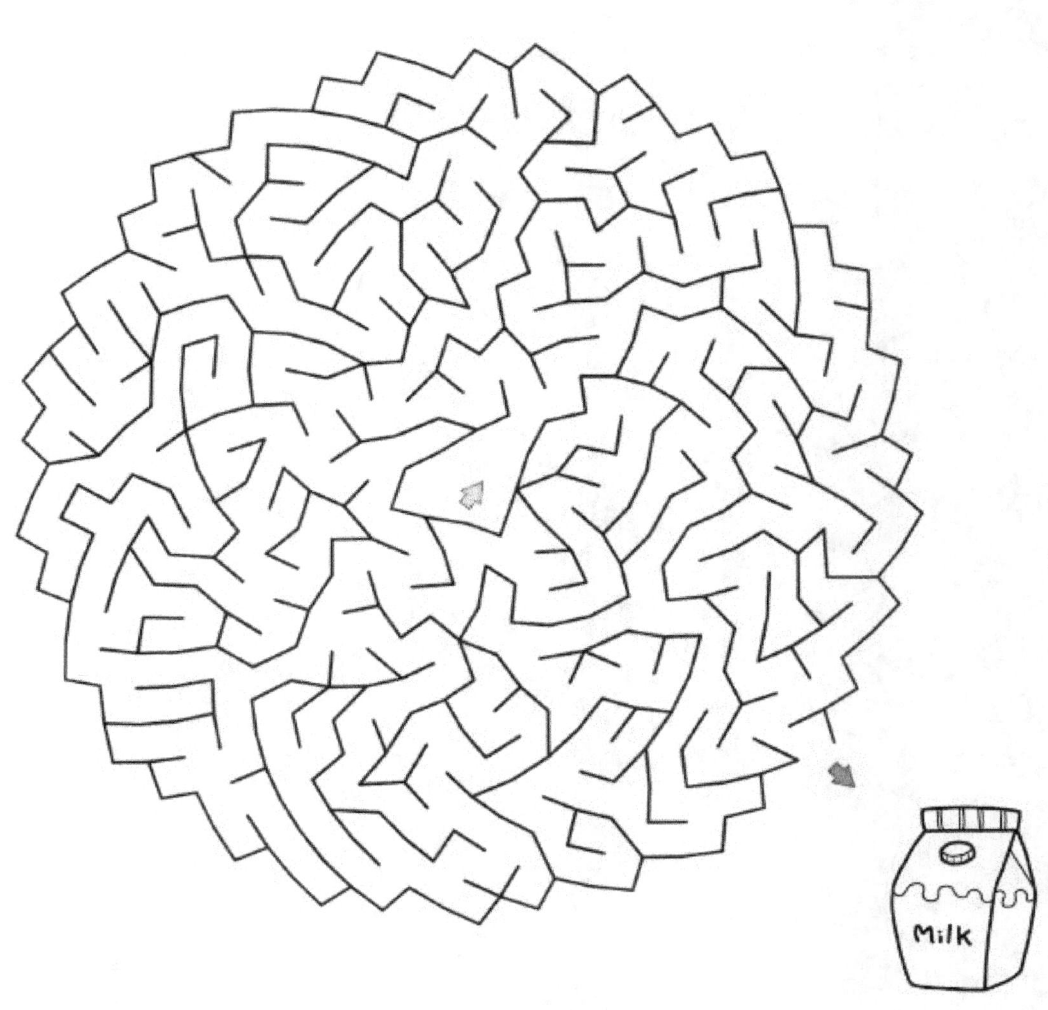

Milk

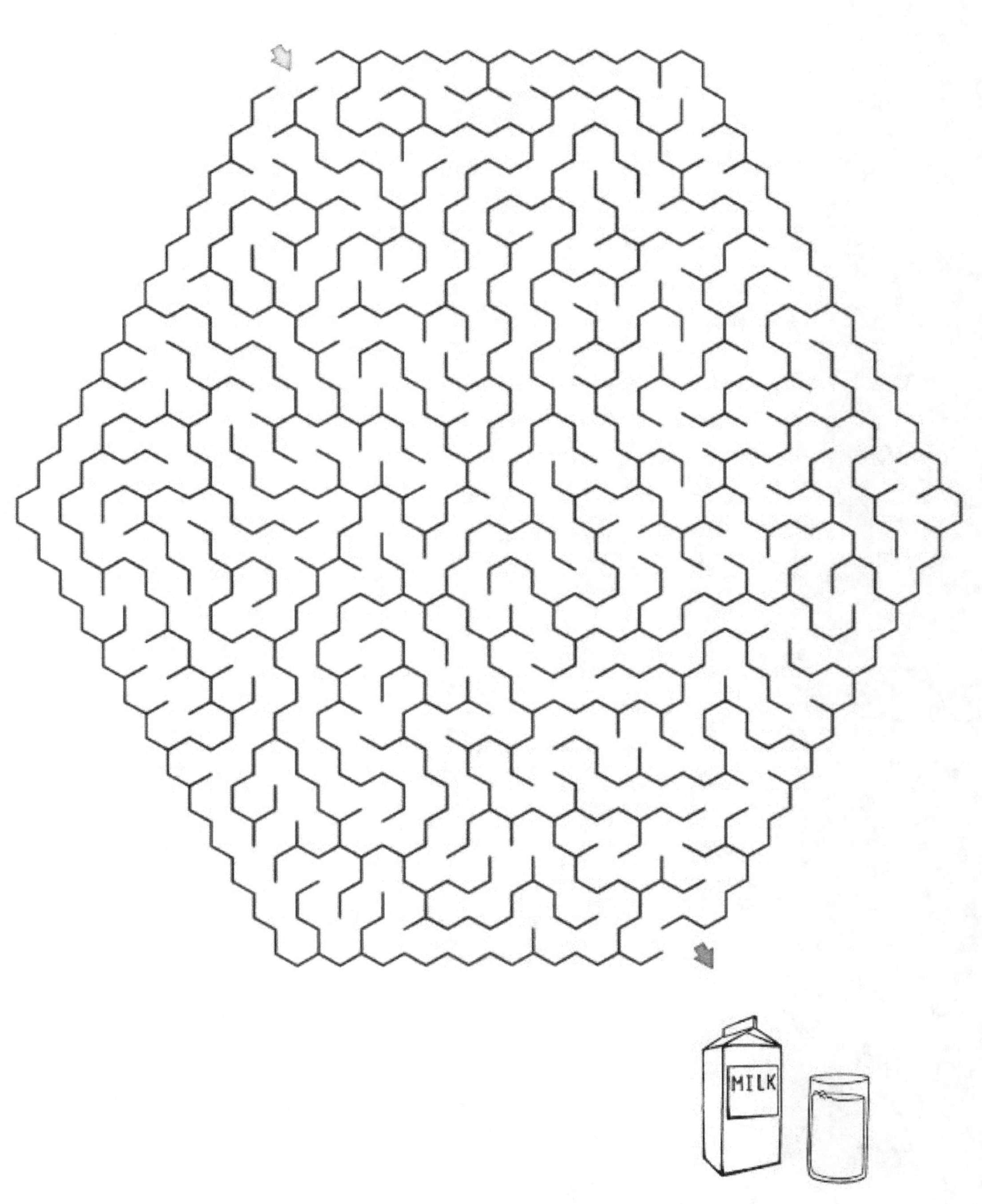

milk

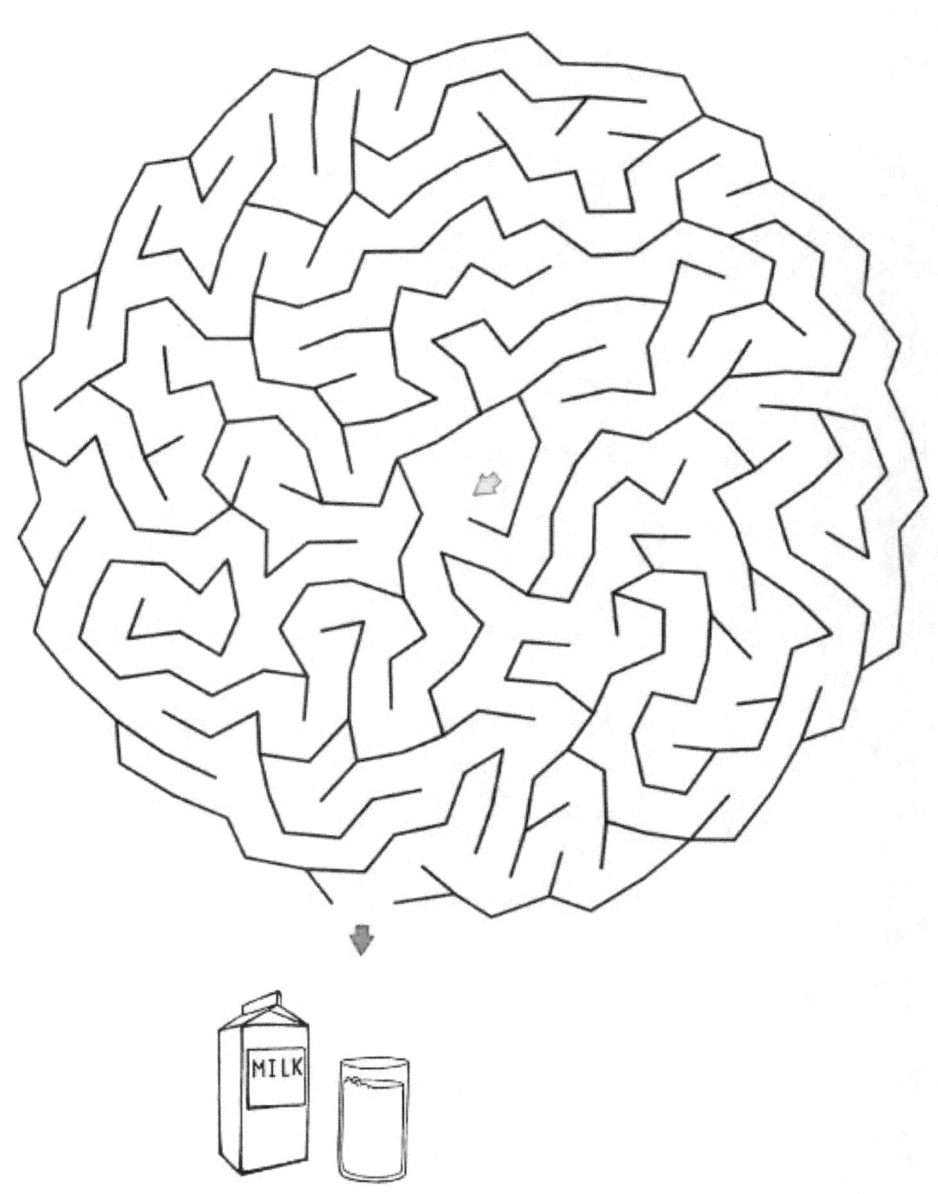
MILK

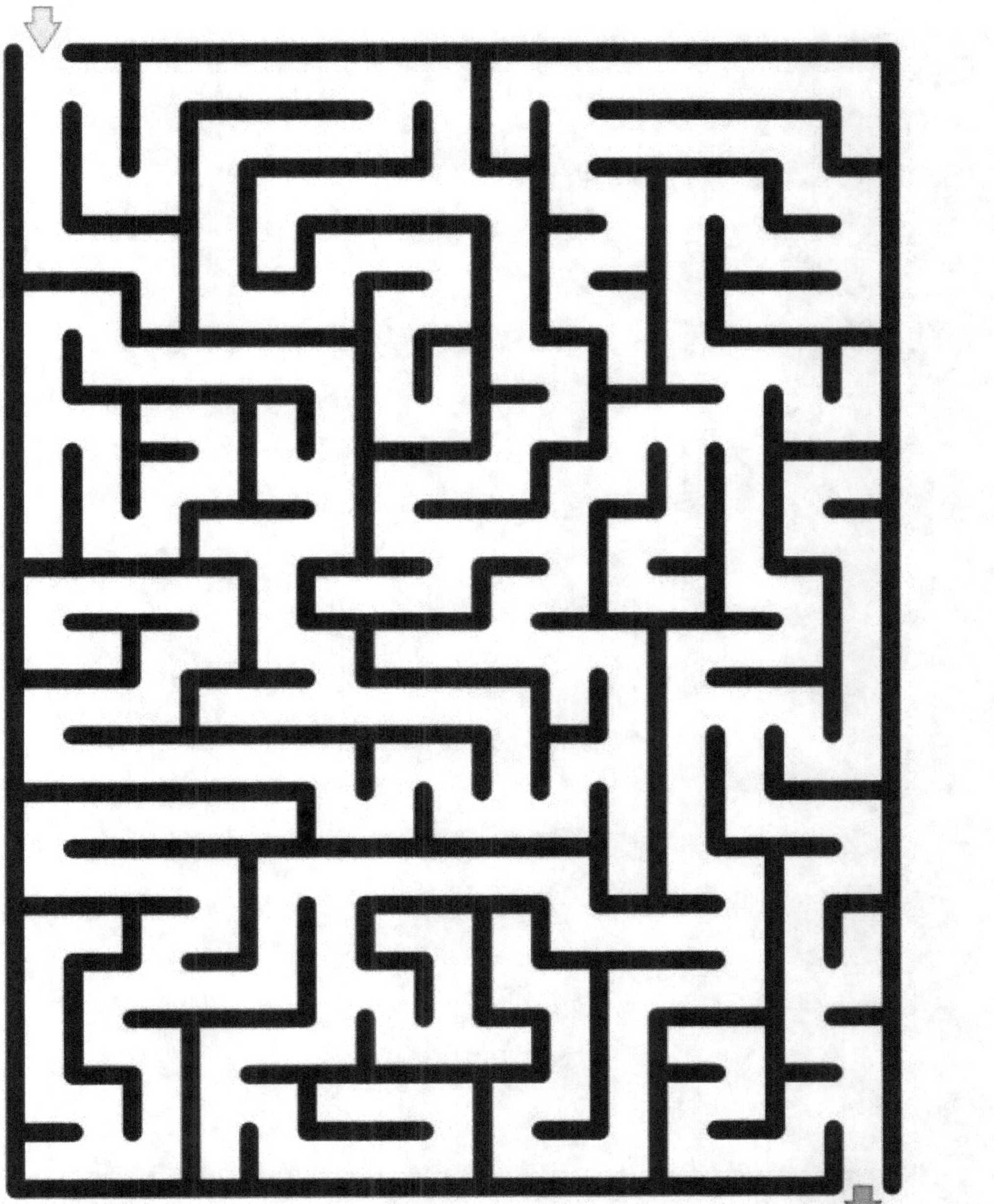

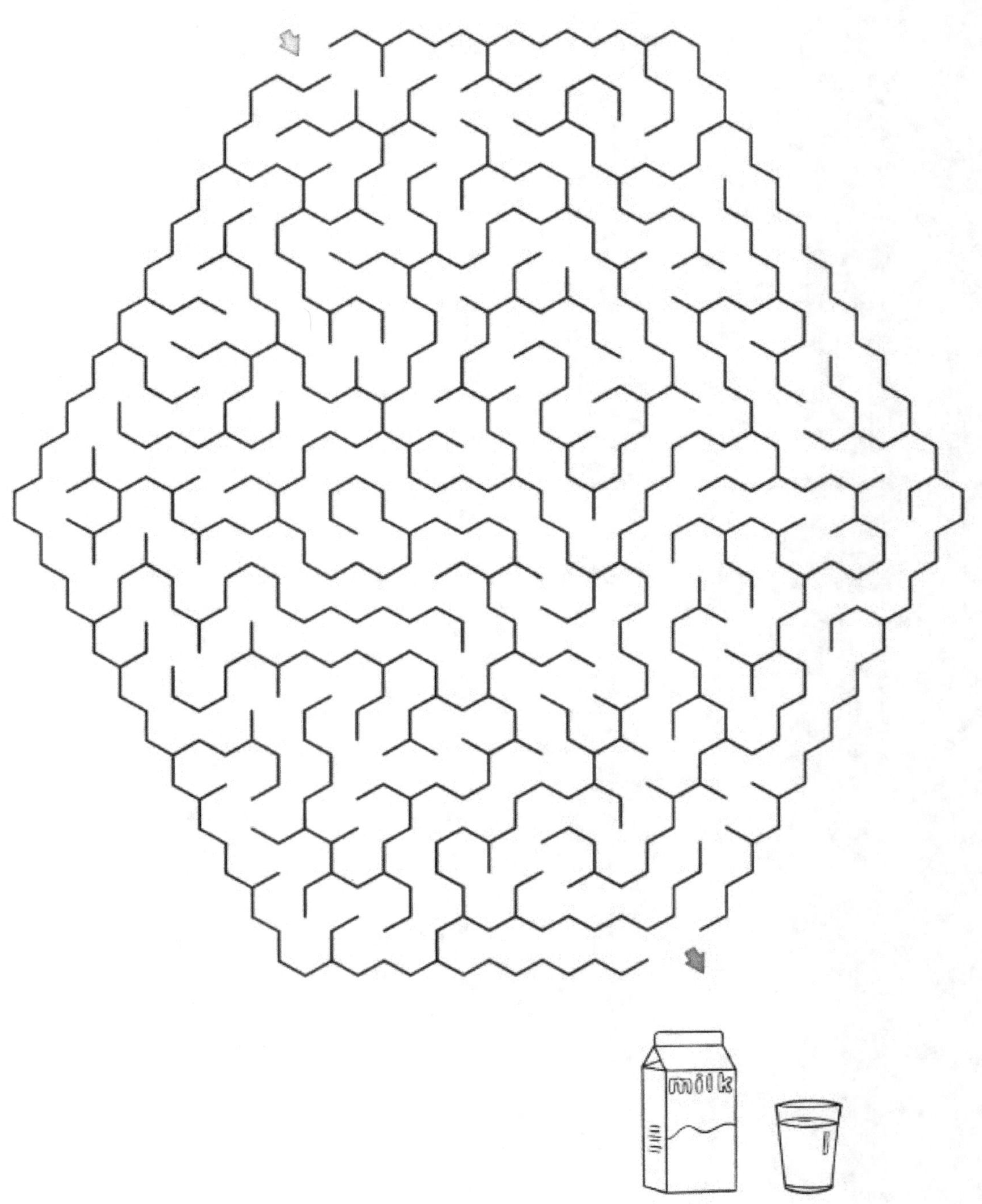

Milk

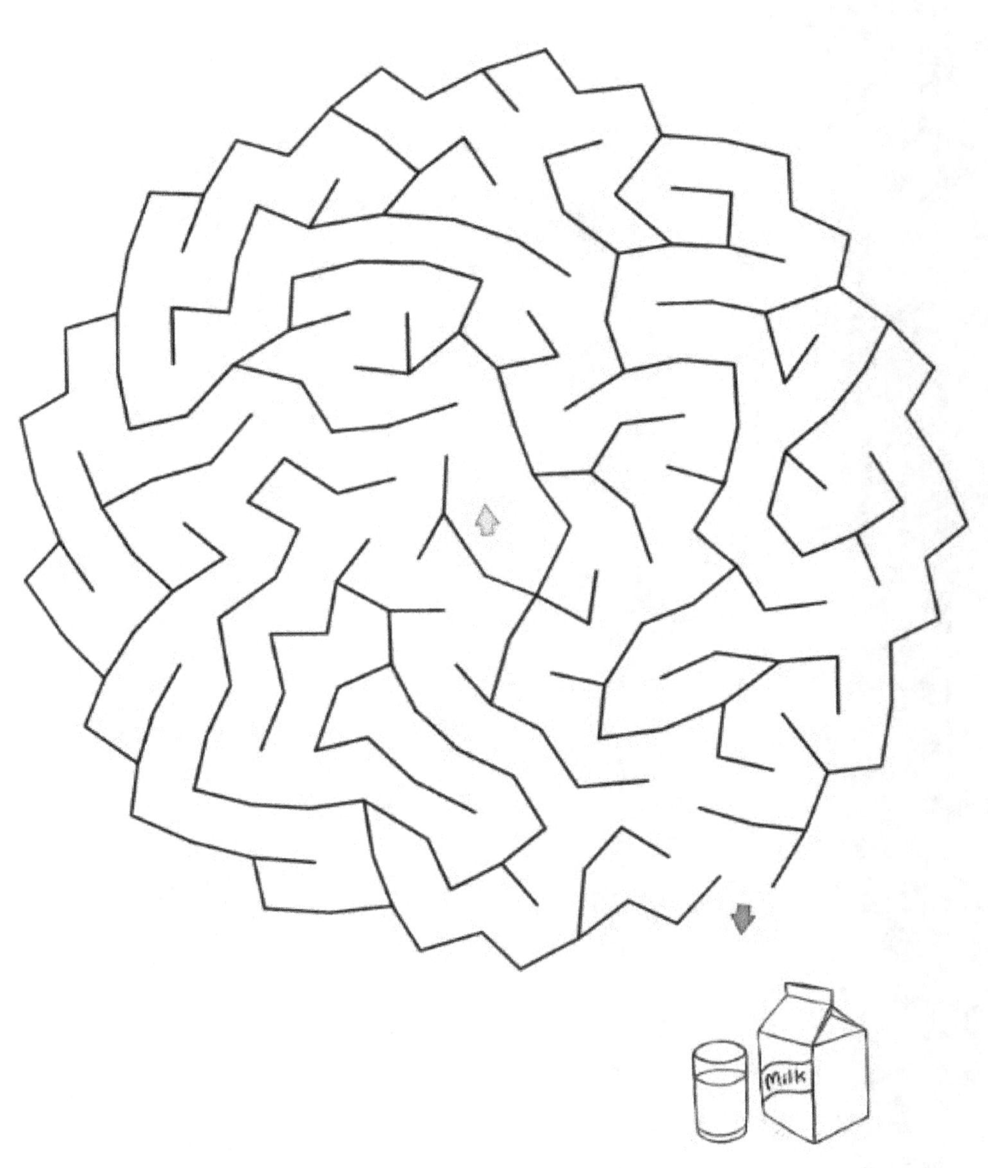

Milk

milk

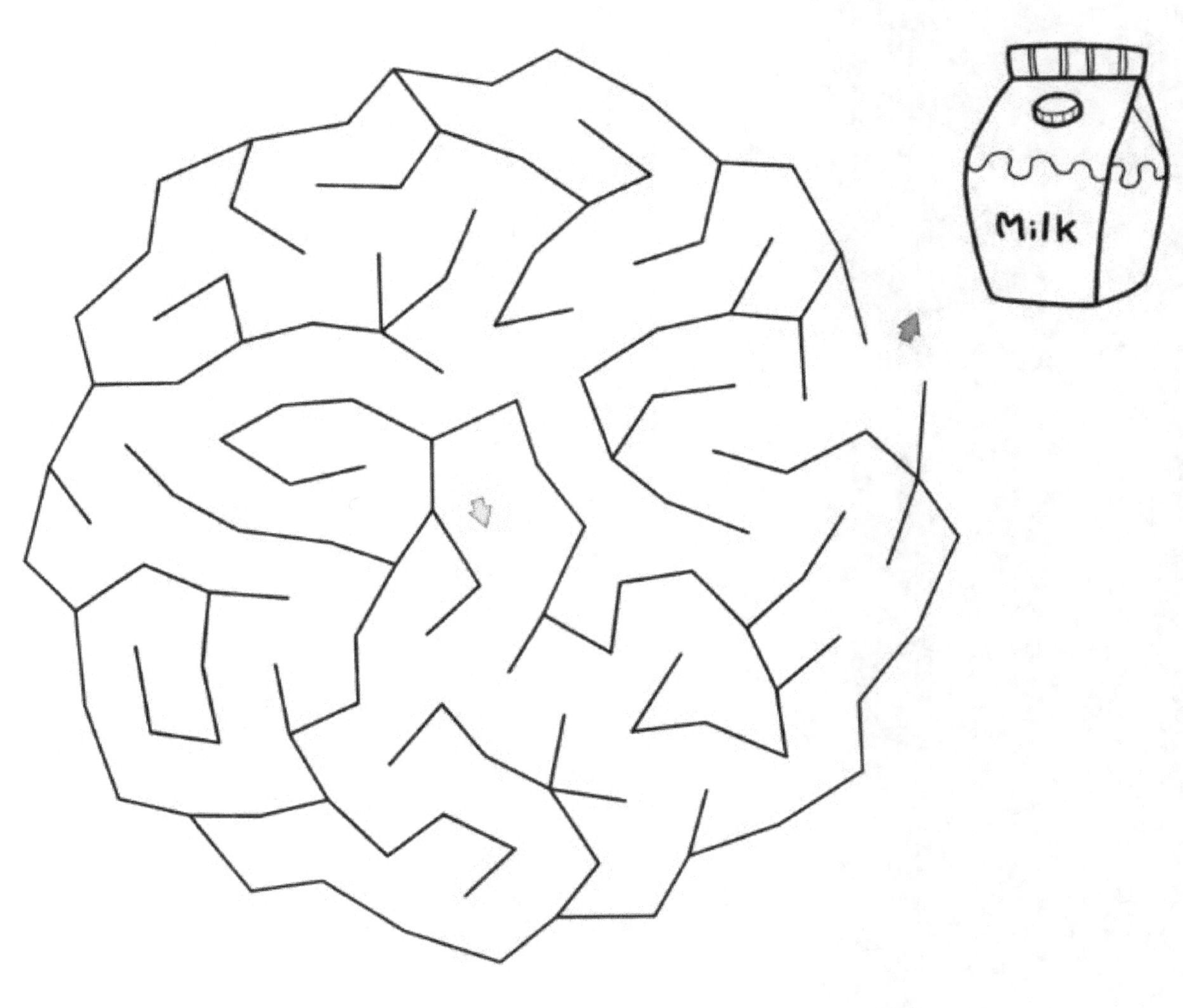

Milk